Music for
ONES and TWOS

Songs and Games for the Very Young Child

	DATE DUE	

Music for ONES and TWOS

Songs and Games for the Very Young Child

by Tom Glazer

Drawings by Karen Ann Weinhaus

A Doubleday Book for Young Readers

For my father (1881–1918), who couldn't stay to see us grow up,
and to the children of the world—and other endangered species.

A Doubleday Book for Young Readers
Published by Delacorte Press
Bantam Doubleday Dell Publishing Group, Inc.
666 Fifth Avenue, New York, New York 10103

Doubleday and the portrayal of an anchor with a dolphin
are trademarks of Bantam Doubleday Dell Publishing Group, Inc.

Library of Congress Catalog Card Number 82-45199
ISBN 0-385-14252-8

Library of Congress Cataloging in Publication Data
Glazer, Tom.
Music for one and twos.
Summary: Fifty-six traditional and original songs,
games, and finger-play rhymes.
1. Singing games.   2. Children's songs.   [1. Songs.
2. Singing games.   3. Games.   4. Finger play.
5. Nursery rhymes]   1. Weinhaus, Karen Ann, ill.
II. Title.
M1993.G54M9   1983   784.6′24′06

Author's Introduction

I have sung for children for over thirty years. An interesting phenomenon has taken place—very gradually, but inexorably, it seems—over that period: the age range of the children attending the concerts has dropped. When I started, it was not too unusual to find young teenagers in the audience occasionally, especially in rural areas. On an NBC radio children's show I co-starred on years ago, our fan mail often included letters from teenagers. Now ten- and eleven-year-olds in my audiences are rarer and rarer; the upper limit seems to be around eight, and I find myself looking longingly for anyone over six.

Was it TV which sophisticated and "adulted" (I almost wrote "adulterated") the child? Perhaps. In any case, along with this new development there arose almost at the same time a more positive and healthy age-level situation: a growing awareness of the importance of educating even babies. Several factors seemed to contribute to focusing more attention on educational devices—music, toys, games, books—at the earliest period in a child's life. I am told by an educator at the Bank Street College of Education in New York that a contributing factor must be the recent massive entrance of mothers into the job market, necessitating the placing of children in day-care centers where, I suppose, educational stimuli are richer, often, than in the home, especially in those homes with limited resources.

I am not a sociologist, a psychoanalyst, a psychiatrist, a psychologist, a social worker, a therapist, or anything much but a wayfaring stranger, so I don't know the reasons for all this. I do know that at this writing my two most popular records by far are for the youngest child—"Let's Sing Fingerplays" and "Music for Ones and Twos" (CMS Records, New York City). Material from the latter record is included in this book.

It is interesting and important, I think, to mention this: over the years, in examining many books and recordings for children, I have noticed that most of the material is written or performed from the point of view of what an *adult* thinks is children's material. It happens, though, that only rarely is the child's own point of view taken into consideration—a child's vocabulary, a child's style of speech, a child's interests. Many prizewinning books (and recordings) for children have been issued that meet with little, or no, interest from the children themselves.

On the other hand, take this line from one of the songs herein: *I roll the ball to Daddy/He rolls the ball to me.* This is as boring to an adult as can be, but it is a thrilling line to a very young child. It emerges directly from the daily life and daily pleasure of a child: his daddy, a ball, rolling the ball back and forth. What could be of greater significance? And, judging by changed attitudes on the part of parents, teachers, librarians, doctors, psychologists, et al., we are more and more appreciating and analyzing the fundamental consequences of the earliest years.

Most of the songs in this book are in book form for the first time, and some are brand new and not on records either. A baker's dozen or so are standard "classics" which we felt could not be omitted even if they have appeared elsewhere. The language of many, but not all, is extremely simple, keeping the child in mind all the time, using mostly one-syllable words. Some songs are a little "older"—but, we hope, fun. The vocabulary varies enormously between the ages of one and two (three- and four-year-olds don't think it untoward to listen to my recording of "Music for Ones and Twos") and varies within the same age group, sometimes very much. But all the songs are geared to the day-to-day life of the child. It is, I suppose, the obverse of the fairy tale; as important as fairy tales are, the daily life of a child is, may I say, perhaps of equal or even greater weight. Here the child hunts no wolf, nor dances the beautiful dance of the sugar-plum fairy; rather, we have songs about a swing, a merry-go-round, a slide, a hammer, taking a bath, being visited by a doctor.

Whitman wrote, "A child said *What is the grass?* fetching it to me with full hands." To answer this question and others children always ask is our duty and obligation and joy. Without adults, children wither and die; without children, adults are not entirely whole, I am certain. I recently was told a *bon mot* in French *"J'aime beaucoup les enfants—des autres."* (I love children very much—other people's.) For those who find it difficult or impossible to like children, I offer another quotation from the French, a children's game song:

> *Dans mon coeur, il n'y a pas d'amour*
> *Mais il y en aura quelque jour.*

Which says roughly, "There is no love in my heart, but there will be someday." I fervently hope so.

Tom Glazer
Beechwood, Scarborough, N.Y.

Using This Material

I have tried to make the piano arrangements simple, though hopefully not simplistic. There are the usual guitar/banjo/autoharp chords. Please don't be dismayed by a key like E♭ or F; it won't be a problem with an autoharp, and you can automatically transpose to the nearest simpler key up or down by attaching a capo to your guitar or banjo. If you encounter chords such as minor sevenths and don't feel confident enough to play them, just approximate them by playing the simple minor—for example, play A minor instead of A minor seventh. In some instances I have indicated alternative chords in parentheses. Sometimes I add a "9" in parentheses to indicate that the actual chord is a ninth; ignore this if you will and play the indicated seventh chord.

If you don't play the guitar or any other chord-making instrument or the piano, don't give up. Pick out the melody alone, if you can, or have someone do it for you. For centuries there has been too much made of the cult of genius in music: we idolize the great ones with such awe and passion that we are embarrassed to make music ourselves. Music should not be made by virtuosi alone. Great poetry needs great audiences, said Walt Whitman. Great audiences, which means you and me, can also be creative. Fred Astaire and Martha Graham and Nureyev are wizard dancers, but there is a unique charm in ordinary people ballroom dancing or square dancing. In short, music, especially for children, can and should be made, in any way, shape, or form. Any music is better than no music at all. Use rhythm instruments if you cannot manage, or have no note-making experience.

I have supplied a few simple lowest-age-level games with no songs. Remember that a game can be made of any children's song, or any other song. Even if you bounce (gently!) a child on your knee or on your lap in time to music, that is a wonderful game in itself, and positively a joyful and stimulating primitive introduction to music. Of course, some of the songs are fingerplay songs with specific instructions for play. But don't be bound by them too strictly. Use this book and the material as a point of departure, not as a bible. Be flexible. Invent. Make up your own games, songs, bits of play. You will be amazed at your hidden creativity when a few inhibitions are dissolved.

I am asked from time to time to speak and demonstrate with children how I use music with them. The first time I was asked to deliver a one-hour lecture on this subject (for the Children's Library Association of Michigan), I began thinking about it almost for the first time, for much of what I have done on the stage for children was pure instinct. I concluded that the quintessential factor underlying it all is simply this: If we love children, we very quickly know what to do with them in teaching or in entertaining them; but if we don't love them, no one can teach us what to do.

Contents

Section IV—More Songs, Songs, Songs

Section V—Some Games

A CHILD'S DAY

What Do We Do?

WORDS AND MUSIC BY RAYMOND ABRASHKIN

*This line changes with each chorus.

2. What do we do at dressing time?
   What do we do at dressing time?
   We put on our clothes, we put on our clothes
   And clap, clap, clap our hands.-*Chorus*

3. What do we do at breakfast time?
   What do we do at breakfast time?
   We drink and eat, we drink and eat
   And clap, clap, clap our hands.-*Chorus*

4. What do we do when we go out?
   What do we do when we go out?
   We dig in the sand, we dig in the sand
   And clap, clap, clap our hands.-*Chorus*

5. What do we do when we come back?
   What do we do when we come back?
   We get in our bath, we get in our bath
   And clap, clap, clap our hands.-*Chorus*

6. What do we do when Daddy comes home?
   What do we do when Daddy comes home?
   We give him a kiss, we give him a kiss
   And clap, clap, clap our hands.-*Chorus*

Where Are Your Eyes?

WORDS AND MUSIC BY RAYMOND ABRASHKIN

1. Where are your eyes? Show me your eyes, Baby's eyes can see. Here are your eyes, here are your eyes, Shut them qui-et-ly.

2. Where are your ears? Show me your ears,
Baby's ears can hear.
These are your ears, these are your ears,
Touch each little ear.

3. Where is your nose? Show me your nose,
Baby's nose can blow.
This is your nose, this is your nose,
Wiggle it just so.

4. Where is your mouth? Show me your mouth,
It can open wide.
Here is your mouth, here is your mouth,
How many teeth inside?

5. Where are your hands? Show me your hands,
   Baby's hands can clap.
   Here are your hands, here are your hands,
   Give a little clap.

6. Where are your feet? Show me your feet,
   Baby's feet are small.
   Here are your feet, here are your feet,
   Kick, kick, kick the ball.

(Spoken) *Now*

7. Shut your eyes, Touch your ears,

Wig - gle your nose, O - pen your mouth,

Clap your hands and Kick, kick, kick. (Spoken) That's all!

What Does Baby See?

WORDS AND MUSIC BY RAYMOND ABRASHKIN

1. Let's look out the window. What do we see? We see a car. Honk! Honk! Hello, car!

1. The car is big, the car is fast, The car can blow its horn. (Honk!) The car goes fast, ver - y fast, Now the car is gone.

2. *Bye-bye, car. Let's look out the window. What do we see? We see a man walking.*
   Hello, man!
3. *Bye-bye, man. Let's look out the window. What do we see? We see a lady. Hello, lady!*

2. A man is walk - ing, step, step, step,
3. A la - dy's walk - ing, tap, tap, tap,

Walk - ing, walk - ing, step by step. A man is walk - ing,
Walk - ing, walk - ing, tap, tap, tap. A la - dy's walk - ing,

step, step, step,
tap, tap, tap, } Walk - ing by our win - dow.

4. Good-bye, lady! Let's look out the window. What do we see? We see a doggy. Hello, doggy!
   Woof! Woof!

4. Lit - tle dog, run, run, run lit - tle dog,

Lit - tle dog, lit - tle dog, run, run, run. Lit - tle dog, lit - tle dog,

run, run, run, Run a - way, run a - way home.

5. *Bye-bye, doggy! Let's look out the window. What do we see? We see a bicycle. Hello, bike!*
6. *Good-bye, bike! Let's look out the window. What do we see? We see another house,*
   with another window, and another child looking at us. Hello there, friend!

5. The bi - cy - cle goes rid - ing by,
6. The bi - cy - cle says, "Ting - a - ling,

Rid - ing by, rid - ing by. The bi - cy - cle goes
Ting - a - ling, ting - a - ling." The bi - cy - cle says,

Rid - ing by,
"Ting - a - ling," } Rid - ing by our win - dow.

What Does Baby Hear?

WORDS AND MUSIC BY RAYMOND ABRASHKIN

1. Listen! What does baby hear? Baby hears the clock.

1. What does the clock say, "Tick - tock, tick - tock," What does the clock say,

"Tick - tock, tick - tock," What does the clock say, "Tick - tock, tick - tock,"

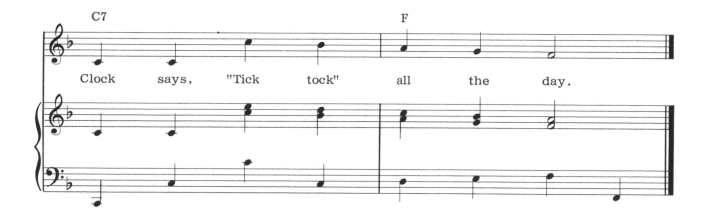

Clock says, "Tick tock" all the day.

Listen! What does baby hear? Baby hears the train.

2. What does the train say, "Choo-choo, choo-choo,"
   What does the train say, "Choo-choo, choo-choo,"
   What does the train say, "Choo-choo, choo-choo,"
   Train says, "Choo-choo" all the day.

Listen! What does baby hear? Baby hears a bell.

3. What does the bell say, "Ding-dong, ding-dong,"
   What does the bell say, "Ding-dong, ding-dong,"
   What does the bell say, "Ding-dong, ding-dong,"
   Bell says, "Ding-dong" all the day.

Listen! What does baby hear? Baby hears a drum.

4. What does the drum say, "Bang-bang, bang-bang,"
   What does the drum say, "Bang-bang, bang-bang,"
   What does the drum say, "Bang-bang, bang-bang,"
   Drum says, "Bang-bang" all the day.

Listen! What does baby hear? Baby hears the water.

5. What does the water say, "Splish-splash, splish-splash,"
   What does the water say, "Splish-splash, splish-splash,"
   What does the water say, "Splish-splash, splish-splash,"
   Water says, "Splish-splash" all the day.

Listen! What does baby hear? Baby hears a horn.

6. What does the horn say, "Toot-toot, toot-toot,"
   What does the horn say, "Toot-toot, toot-toot,"
   What does the horn say, "Toot-toot, toot-toot,"
   Horn says, "Toot-toot" all the day.

Baby's Going Bye-Bye

WORDS AND MUSIC BY RAYMOND ABRASHKIN

1. *Mother's work is finished. The sun is shining and it's time to get dressed and go bye-bye.*
2. *Now baby's shoes are on, but baby is not ready yet.*

Now baby's shoes and coat are on, but baby is not ready yet.

3. Baby's going bye-bye; put on baby's mittens.
   One hand, one mitten, find the thumb,
   Other hand, other mitten, other thumb.

Now baby's shoes and coat and mittens are on, but baby is not ready yet.

4. Baby's going bye-bye; where is baby's hat?
    Sit, take it, put it on,
    Hold still, there now, it's all done.

Now baby's shoes and coat and mittens and hat are on, and baby's ready . . .

5. Baby's going bye-bye; baby's ready now.
    Hurry, hurry, 'cross the floor,
    Go out, right out, through the door.

Now, baby's going bye-bye!

6. Baby's going bye-bye; what will baby see?
    Outside we see trees and sky.
    Then stop. *(Pause)* Then turn. *(Pause)*
    Wave bye-bye,

Finale: *Bye-bye, wave bye-bye.*

Finale [end of 6th verse only]

23

Baby Doll

WORDS AND MUSIC BY RAYMOND ABRASHKIN

Doll says, "Mama, Mama." Baby doll says, "Mama, Mama." Nice doll, pretty doll . . .

I Rock My Doll

WORDS AND MUSIC BY RAYMOND ABRASHKIN

And now, rock your dolly to sleep.

Blocks

WORDS AND MUSIC BY RAYMOND ABRASHKIN

I Roll the Ball

WORDS AND MUSIC BY RAYMOND ABRASHKIN

Listen to the Noises

WORDS AND MUSIC BY RAYMOND ABRASHKIN

A real fire engine is very big.
A real fire engine makes a very big noise: WHE-E-E-E-E!
My fire engine is very little.
My fire engine makes a very little noise: whe-e-e-e...

A real boat whistle makes a big noise: WHO-O-O-O-O!
My toy whistle makes a very little noise: who-o-o-o-o...

My Daddy's and Mommy's hammer makes a big noise: CLUNK, CLUNK, CLUNK!
My little hammer makes a little noise: click, click, click...

The lion in the zoo makes a big noise: ROAR-R-R-R!
My little pussy cat makes a little noise: meouw, meouw...

A big drum makes a big noise: BOOM, BOOM, BOOM-BOOM-BOOM!
My little drum makes a little noise: tap, tap, tap-tap-tap...

My Daddy has big hands.
My Daddy's hands make a big clap: CLAP, CLAP, CLAP!
I have little hands.
My hands make a little clap: clap, clap, clap...

(Repeat song.)

Up in the Air

WORDS AND MUSIC BY RAYMOND ABRASHKIN

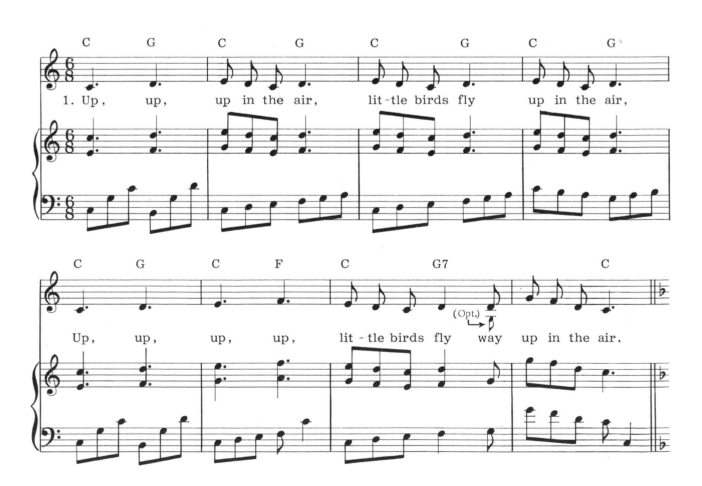

1. Up, up, up in the air, lit-tle birds fly up in the air,

Up, up, up, up, lit-tle birds fly way up in the air.

Dad-dy picks ba - by up in the air. Up, up, up in the air.
[Mom-my]

Ba-by can fly like a bird in the sky, High up, high up in the air.

2. Up, up, up in the air; trees grow way up in the air,
Up, up, up, up, trees grow way up, way up in the air.
Daddy picks baby up in the air, up, up, up in the air.
Baby can be just as tall as a tree,
High up, high up in the air.

3. Up, up, up in the air; air-o-plane goes way up in the air,
Up, up, up in the air; air-o-plane goes way up in the air.
Daddy picks baby up in the air, up, up, up in the air.
Baby can go like a plane flying so,
High up, high up in the air.

4. Up, up, up in the air; smoke goes way up, up in the air,
Up, up, up in the air; smoke goes way up, up in the air.
Daddy picks baby up in the air, up, up, up in the air.
Now baby goes where the smoke always blows,
High up, high up in the air.

5. (Last time, half-chorus only)
Up, up, up in the air; Daddy picks baby up in the air,
Up, up, up, up, and Daddy puts baby down in the chair.

The Bath

WORDS AND MUSIC BY RAYMOND ABRASHKIN

Listen! Water is running into the bathtub. Give baby a hug. Take off baby's clothes, and into the tub baby now goes. Splash! Splash!
1. Now, hold up your hands.

1. Ba - by, ba - by, wash your hands; ba - by's bath is fun.____

Ba - by, ba - by, wash your hands, now your hands are done.____

Next, hold up your feet.

2. Baby, baby, wash your toes; baby's bath is fun.
   Baby, baby, wash your toes; now your toes are done.

Next, hold up your face and close your eyes.

3. Baby, baby, wash your face; baby's bath is fun.
   Baby, baby, wash your face; now your face is done.

   (or use nose, ears, cheeks, etc.)

Now, stand up, please.

4. Baby, baby, wash your back; baby's bath is fun.
   Baby, baby, wash your back; now your back is done.

Now, turn around, please.

5. Baby, baby, wash your front; baby's bath is fun.
   Baby, baby, wash your front; now your front is done.

Now, baby is all washed, and . . .

6. Baby, baby, here's your towel; baby's bath is fun.
   Baby, baby, here's your towel; now your bath is done.

Where Can Baby Be?

WORDS AND MUSIC BY RAYMOND ABRASHKIN

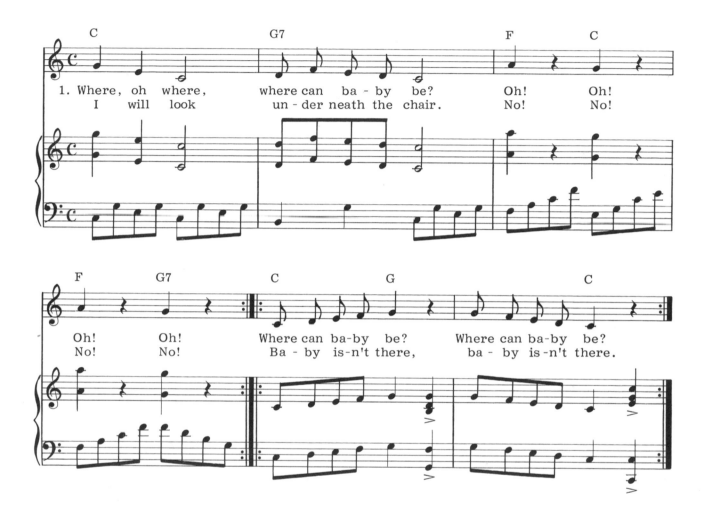

2. Where, oh where, where can baby be? Oh! Oh! Oh! Oh!
I will look all along the wall. No! No! No! No!
Where can baby be? Where can baby be?
No one's there at all, no one's there at all.

3. Where, oh where, where can baby be? Oh! Oh! Oh! Oh!
I will look outside in the hall. No! No! No! No!
Where can baby be? Where can baby be?
No one's there at all, no one's there at all.

4. Where, oh where, where can baby be? Oh! Oh! Oh! Oh!
I will go look in baby's bed. Oh! Oh! Oh! Oh!
I see a little head, I see a little head.

5. Someone's here, and I wonder who? Yes, Yes—Yes, Yes
Now I can see you
Peek-a, peek-a-boo; (Spoken) *Peek-a-boo!*
(No repeats in fifth verse)

Sleeping Time

WORDS AND MUSIC BY RAYMOND ABRASHKIN

Lit-tle bun-nies and lambs are home for the night, Ba-by birds in their nests are, too. Lit-tle kit-tens and chicks are go-ing to sleep, And so are you.

Good Night

WORDS AND MUSIC BY RAYMOND ABRASHKIN

The Shiny Silver Moon

WORDS AND MUSIC BY RAYMOND ABRASHKIN

Now snuggle down nice and warm and close your eyes.

The shin-y sil-ver moon floats a-cross the sky. It's
mor-row will be yours, lit-tle one, to keep, But

sleep-ing time for ba-bies, close your eyes. No more time is
now to-day is o-ver, go to sleep.

left to play, All your toys are put a-way. To-

* Hold last time only.

Section II

THE PLAYGROUND

The Swing

WORDS: ROBERT LOUIS STEVENSON   MUSIC: TOM GLAZER

3. Till I look down on the garden green,
Down on the roof so brown—
Up in the air I go flying again,
Up in the air and down!

The Squirrel

WORDS AND MUSIC BY TOM GLAZER

A squirrel is in the playground. He has a long tail. He runs fast. We feed him. He likes that.

2. Nibble, nibble, nibble on an acorn brown,
   Dribble, dribble, dribble and the shells all around.
   Hop, skip, jump in the great oak tree,
   Wish that I was him and he was me.

3. Up in the green tree, down on the hill,
   Over the meadow, never still,
   Chitter, chatter chatter till the sun goes down,
   Nibble, nibble, nibble on an acorn brown.

If I Could Fly

WORDS AND MUSIC BY TOM GLAZER

We feed birds, too. Hi, birds. Don't fly away. I will feed you. Sing, birds. Sing.
Here is corn, birds.

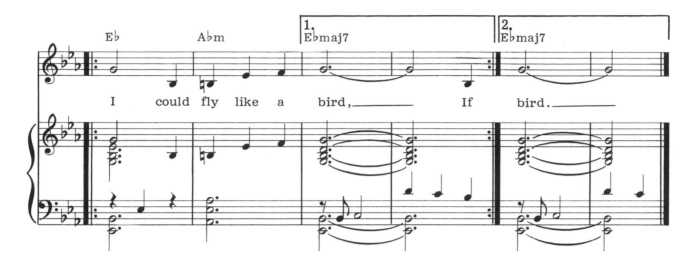

2. If I could fly like a bird,
   I'd say hello to a kite,
   And look inside chimney tops,
   And howl at owls in the night.

3. If I could fly like a bird,
   I'd sit on a very high tree,
   And peek in a robin's nest,
   And all would look up to me.
   If I could fly like a bird,
   If I could fly like a bird.

The Sandbox

WORDS AND MUSIC BY TOM GLAZER

Here is the sandbox. I sit in it. I make sand castles in it. The sand runs out of my fingers. It can be hard. It can be soft.

2. I can make a mountain bigger than yours,
I can make a castle taller than yours,
I can build a building higher than yours,
I can make a sandman sandier than yours.

Chorus: Playing in my sandbox, look at me!
Sand in my shoes 'n' socks, look at me!
Shovel in my bucket, lollipop, I'll suck it,
Playing in my sandbox, look at me!

The Jungle Gym

WORDS AND MUSIC BY TOM GLAZER

The Balloon

WORDS AND MUSIC BY TOM GLAZER

A man has balloons in the playground. Red, blue, yellow, green, orange balloons. He gives me one. If I don't hold it, it flies away.

Very gently and softly

1. I wish that I were a red bal-loon,
2. I'd say hel-lo to a friend-ly bird,

Float - ing free si - lent - ly, Tied to the fin - ger of
Go - ing by way up high, I'd pull me down when the

me my - self, Ly - ing in the grass.
sun had set, Me and my bal - loon.

The Merry-Go-Round

WORDS AND MUSIC BY TOM GLAZER

The Slide

WORDS AND MUSIC BY TOM GLAZER

Put me on the slide, Mom. On the slide, Dad. Watch me. Whoosh! Down. Fast! Whee!

1. I love it when I go slid - ing, It's
2. Then I go to the top a - gain, And I

ver - y, ver - y ex - cit - ing, I slide on my
slide right down a - gain. I say, "Look, Ma, no

bot - tom To get to the bot - tom.
hands, I use the seat of my pants."

The See-Saw

WORDS AND MUSIC BY TOM GLAZER

Slowly (See-saw rhythm)

1. I see you see we see the see - saw, tra - la - la.
2. I'm up you're down, you're up and I'm down, ha, ha, ha.

Don't push too hard, don't be push - y,

Don't push too hard, I'll hurt my toosh - ie. I saw,

you saw, we saw the see - saw, tra - la - la.

SECTION III

FAVORITE FINGERPLAYS

Pat-a-Cake

WORDS: ANON.   MUSIC: TOM GLAZER

Can be done alone or in pairs, moving the hands of the child. Pat the hands twice in the first measure, on the first and third beat; three times in the second measure, on the first, second, and third beat, following the tune. The same with measures three and four. Make a rolling motion on "roll it," than a pat and write "B," then throw arms out on last line.

What Will We Do with the Baby-O?

WORDS AND MUSIC ADAPTED BY TOM GLAZER

1. What will we do with the ba - by - o? What will we do with the ba - by - o?
2. Wind blows high and the wind blows low, Where, oh where does the old wind go?

What will we do with the ba - by - o? Send him to his Dad - dy - o.
What will we do with the ba - by - o? Send him to his Dad - dy - o.

3. Down in the hollow the cowbells ring,
   Bullfrogs jump and the jaybirds sing.
   What will we do with the baby-o?
   Send him to his Daddy-o.

4. Bullfrog croaked and jumped up high,
   Jumped and jumped till he caught a fly.
   What will we do with the baby-o?
   Send him to his Daddy-o.

v.1. Pantomime rocking a baby in arms in tempo.
v.2. Throw arms out and up on "high," and in and down on "low"; repeat through
     rest of verse.
v.3. Point to a hollow and ring a bell. Close fist and throw up high; move fingers
     back and forth against thumb to imitate birds singing.
v.4. Using fist for bullfrog, act out the words as indicated.

I'm a Little Teapot

WRITTEN BY CLARENCE KELLEY AND GEORGE SANDERS

1. I'm a lit-tle tea-pot short and stout, Here is my han-dle, here is my spout.
2. I'm a ver-y spe-cial pot it's true, Here, let me show you what I can do.

When I get all steamed up then I shout, Tip me o-ver and pour me out.
I can change my han-dle and my spout, Tip me o-ver and pour me out.

v.1. Act very stout. Place one hand on hip. Extend other arm, elbow and wrist bent. Nod head vigorously. Tip sideways in direction of extended arm.

v.2. Reverse hand on hip and extended arm, and tip in the other direction.

Here Is the Church

WORDS: ANON. MUSIC: TOM GLAZER

Here is the church, here is the stee-ple, O-pen the doors and see all the peo-ple. Here is the par-son go-ing up-stairs, And here he is a-say-ing his prayers.

Each play of the fingers comes after each phrase of the song.
1. Interlace fingers with fingertips down and knuckles showing.
2. Unfold forefingers only to form an inverted "V" like a steeple.
3. Turn palms upward showing interlaced fingertips.
4. Wiggle interlaced fingers.
5. Unlace fingers. Form a "ladder" with one hand, fingers apart, and climb up ladder with first two fingers of other hand.
6. Form hands pointing upward together in a praying position.

Shoo Fly

WORDS AND MUSIC: ANON.

Shoo fly, don't both - er me, shoo fly, don't both - er me!

Shoo fly, don't both er me, for I be-long to some-bod-y. I

feel, I feel, I feel like a morn-ing star, I feel, I

1. feel, I feel like a morn-ing star. 2. Oh feel like a morn-ing star.

In a dismissal gesture, raise both hands, palms out, and push, on the words "Shoo fly." Then, on "don't bother me," return hands to thighs as you sit, slapping the thighs with your palms in rhythm. When you get to the words "I feel," hug yourself to the end, then repeat at will.

Lazy Mary

WORDS AND MUSIC: ANON.

v.1. Point an admonishing finger in rhythm.
v.2. Shake the head negatively, again in rhythm, throughout the entire verse.
Then repeat ad lib.

Bingo

WORDS AND MUSIC: ANON.

A fine way to begin learning letters. Slowing the song down for this purpose, have the children "write" each letter named in the song.

Eentsy Weentsy Spider

ADAPTED BY TOM GLAZER

For babies, simply "climb" up and down the baby's arm or body (gently!), using two fingers in a walking motion.

For children old enough to imitate or take directions, place each thumb against forefinger of the other hand, then swivel the fingers alternately so that one thumb-and-forefinger pair goes above, followed by the second pair, making a motion as if climbing, though the fingers remain in the same place. This on line one. On line two, drop the arms to the side while the fingers wiggle. On line three, make a big circle with the hands clasped over the head, to show the sun. The last line repeats the first.

Ten Fingers

WORDS: ADAPTED BY TOM GLAZER   MUSIC: TOM GLAZER

Rather slow

1. I have ten lit - tle fin - gers and they all be - long to me,_____
2. I can shut them up_____ tight or o - pen them wide, I can

I can make them do things, would you like_ to see?_____
Put them all to - geth - er, or make_____ them_ all hide._____

3. I can make them jump high, I can make them jump low,

I can fold_them qui - et - ly and hold them just so._____

60   Hold hands up Show ten fingers and suit actions to the words.

Hickory, Dickory, Dock

WORDS: ANON.　　　　MUSIC: TOM GLAZER

On "Hickory, dickory, dock," take the child's hands and clap them together softly in rhythm. "Run" with your two fingers up the child's arm. On "The clock struck one," close one hand with a forefinger straight up, for "one," then run down the child's arm on the next phrase. On the last phrase repeat the first, clapping the child's hands in your own rhythmically.

This Little Pig

WORDS: ANON.   MUSIC: TOM GLAZER

The traditional way is merely to sing the song or say the words, holding or pointing to each of the child's fingers, starting with the thumb. On "Wee, wee, wee," gently tickle the child.

One Finger, One Thumb

ADAPTED BY TOM GLAZER

*Keep adding things here, as verses proceed.

3. One finger, one thumb, two hands, keep moving,
One finger, one thumb, two hands, keep moving,
One finger, one thumb, two hands, keep moving,
And we'll all be happy and gay.

4. One finger, one thumb, one arm, keep moving,
One finger, one thumb, one arm, keep moving,
One finger, one thumb, one arm, keep moving,
And we'll all be happy and gay.

5. One finger, one thumb, two arms, keep moving,
One finger, one thumb, two arms, keep moving,
One finger, one thumb, two arms, keep moving,
And we'll all be happy and gay.

6. One finger, one thumb, one leg, keep moving,
One finger, one thumb, one leg, keep moving,
One finger, one thumb, one leg, keep moving,
And we'll all be happy and gay.

7. One finger, one thumb, two legs, keep moving,
One finger, one thumb, two legs, keep moving,
One finger, one thumb, two legs, keep moving,
And we'll all be happy and gay.

8. One finger, one thumb, get up, keep moving,
One finger, one thumb, get up, keep moving,
One finger, one thumb, get up, keep moving,
And we'll all be happy and gay.

9. One finger, one thumb, sit down, keep moving,
One finger, one thumb, sit down, keep moving,
One finger, one thumb, sit down, keep moving,
And we'll all be happy and gay.

Suit the action to the words. Note that the verses are cumulative—that is, all the
preceding verses are repeated with each subsequent verse.

Where Is Thumbkin?

WORDS AND MUSIC: ANON.

3. Where is middle? Where is middle?
Here I am, here I am;
How are you today, sir?
Very well, I thank you,
Run away, run away.

4. Where is ringer? Where is ringer?
Here I am, here I am;
How are you today, sir?
Very well, I thank you,
Run away, run away.

5. Where is pinky? Where is pinky?
   Here I am, here I am;
   How are you today, sir?
   Very well, I thank you,
   Run away, run away.

Place hands behind back. Show one thumb, then the other on the words "Here I am, here I am." Bend one thumb, then the other. Wiggle thumbs and move hands away from the body. The rest of the song follows the same pattern, using a different finger (both hands) each time, the actions coordinating with the words.

Bye, Baby Bunting

ADAPTED BY TOM GLAZER

1. Bye, Baby Bunting, Daddy's gone a-hunting, To get a little rabbit skin, To wrap his Baby Bunting in._____

2. Bye, Baby Bunting, Mommy's gone a-hunting, To find a little safety pin, To fasten baby's diaper in._____

v.1. Wave bye-bye. Hold an imaginary rifle, one arm extended, the other bent with fist under the eye. Hold arms up before face, hands bent a little, "holding a skin." Rock a baby in your arms.

v.2. Wave bye-bye. Hold rifle. Open and close a forefinger against thumb. Pat pretend baby—or a real one.

Section IV

MORE SONGS, SONGS, SONGS

Cradle Song

WORDS: TOM GLAZER   MUSIC: JOHANNES BRAHMS

1.Lul-la - by and good night, may your
by and good night, guard-ian

dreams be of ros - es, And of sug - ar and__ spice and__
an - gels at - tend you; In the shad - ows of__ stars may the

ev - 'ry-thing that's nice. Day will break, may you wake to a
trou-bled night wind cease. While the moon is a - wake may the

world full of ros - es. Day will break, may you wake to a
good Lord de - fend you. While the moon is a - wake may the

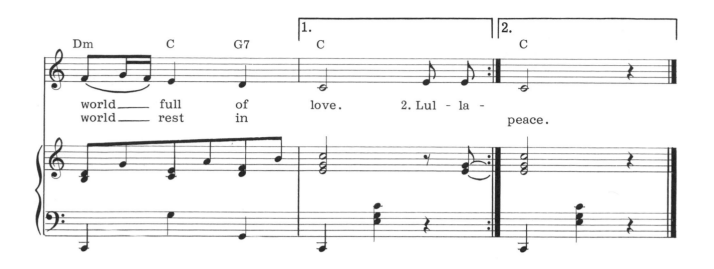

world___ full of love. 2. Lul - la -
world___ rest in peace.

If this—the most beautiful, perhaps, of all cradle songs—doesn't put a child to sleep, then the child at least has been exposed to the musical genius of Johannes Brahms, so you win either way.

All the Pretty Little Horses

ADAPTED BY TOM GLAZER

Go to sleep-y, lit-tle ba — by,

When you wake I'll give you some cake;

All the pret-ty lit-tle hors — es, hors — es.

1. Lit - tle brown ones, lit - tle red ones, All the pret-ty lit-tle

2. Lit - tle blue ones, lit - tle green ones, All the pret-ty lit-tle

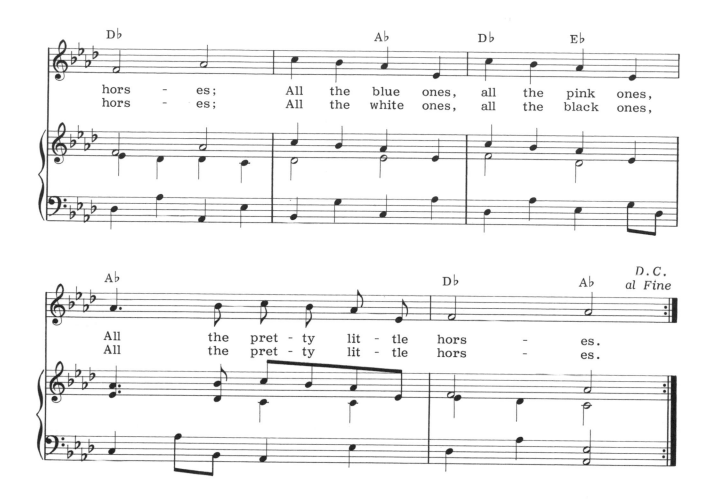

The best thing to do with this lovely song is either to have the child pretend to take a nap—children love doing that for a few moments—or to use it as a lullaby in a real going-to-sleep situation. If the child has a doll, the pretending, of course, can be directed to the doll as child and the doll's owner as parent.

Don't You Push Me Down

WORDS AND MUSIC BY WOODY GUTHRIE

Well you can play with me, and you can hold my hand.

We can skip to - geth - er down to the ice-cream man. You can

wear my Mom - my's shoes, put on my Dad - dy's hat.

You can e - ven laugh at me, but don't you push me down.

Chorus

Don't you push me, push me, push me, don't you push me down,

Don't you push me, push me, push me, don't you push me down.

Little Peter Rabbit

WORDS AND MUSIC ADAPTED BY TOM GLAZER

A fly. Flew. On my. Nose! I flicked it. Came back. Flicked it. Came back. Again. Again.
Fly away, fly. Away. Away. Away.

flicked it and it flew a - way.

2. Little Sally Squirrel had a wart upon her knee,
   Little Sally Squirrel had a wart upon her knee,
   Little Sally Squirrel had a wart upon her knee;
   With milkweed it went right away.

3. Little Charley Chipmunk had a bug upon his belly button,
   Little Charley Chipmunk had a bug upon his belly button,
   Little Charley Chipmunk had a bug upon his belly button;
   He bugged it and it crawled away.

4. Little Rose Raccoon had a worm between her toes,
   Little Rose Raccoon had a worm between her toes,
   Little Rose Raccoon had a worm between her toes;
   She tickled it and it went away.

5. Little Mickey Mole had a hole in his doughnut,
   Little Mickey Mole had a hole in his doughnut,
   Little Mickey Mole had a hole in his doughnut;
   He ate it and it went away.

6. Little Danny Dragon had mosquitoes on his scales,
   Little Danny Dragon had mosquitoes on his scales,
   Little Danny Dragon had mosquitoes on his scales;
   He weighed them and they went a-weigh.

7. Little Fanny Flea had a dinosaur on her eyebrow,
   Little Fanny Flea had a dinosaur on her eyebrow,
   Little Fanny Flea had a dinosaur on her eyebrow;
   She winged it and it went away.

The Zoo

WORDS AND MUSIC BY TOM GLAZER

Here is the zoo. Here is a lion. Here is an elephant. Here is a flamingo. Here is a camel.
A fox. Lots more!

1. There is a zoo, I'm go-ing to, With Mom and
li-on, he was-n't cry-in', He was-n't

Dad, and I'm so glad. 2. I saw a
roar-in', but he was snor-in'. 3. I saw a

min - go,   so bright and pink - o,   He looked like
fox, __   locked in a box __   They called a

Ring - o,   but could not sing - o.   8. I saw a
cage; __   I felt his   rage.   9. I saw a

· seal,   oh, real - ly real,   Fed him a kip - per;   he flapped his

flip - per.   10. I told the an - i - mals   in the

Ad lib. (Slower)

80

zoo,   If you don't eat me,   I won't eat you!

I Had a Little Rooster (The Greenberry Tree)

WORDS AND MUSIC ADAPTED BY TOM GLAZER

* From the second verse on, repeat third line of all preceding verses before singing last line.

3. I had a little duck, and the duck pleased me.
   I fed my duck on the greenberry tree.
   That little duck said, quack, quack, quack,(The little hen said,...*etc.*)
   De doodle, de doodle, de doodle de doo.

4. I had a little dog, and the dog pleased me.
   I fed my dog on the greenberry tree.
   That little dog said, bow, wow, wow,(The little duck said,...*etc.*)
   De doodle, de doodle, de doodle de doo.

5.—1,000,000.: Add your own animules!

I Got a Camel for Christmas

WORDS AND MUSIC BY TOM GLAZER

A camel? Honest? For Christmas? You're fibbing, aren't you? No? Not a camel?
For Christmas!!

I got a cam-el for Christ-mas, oh how my heart did jump! The rea-son was be-cause old San-ta Claus was slid-ing up and down his hump. When Ma-ma saw my cam-el, she

G7

pants,   they were laugh-ing so   hard   in the school yard.   So I

C   F   F7

named my cam - el   Sam-'l,___   and I   rode him to school in-stead of the

Gm   Bm7♭5(G7)   G7   Dm7   Fm(6)   C   C♯o

bus (leave the driv-ing to   us). And ev-'ry-thing was fine till   next Christ-mas

Dm7   D7(9)   G7   C

time when San - ta sent   me   a   hip - po-pot - a -mus!___

Where Go the Boats? (Dark Brown Is the River)

WORDS: R.L. STEVENSON   MUSIC: ADAPTED BY TOM GLAZER

Doctor, Doctor

WORDS AND MUSIC BY TOM GLAZER

I feel icky. I am in bed. I am not hungry. I am not thirsty. I am not anything. I am SICK,
SICK, SICK! Darn it! I can't play. My dose is rudding. My head is hot. Mommy says I
have a temp-a-choor. A temp-a-what? I got a code in my dose. I blow. I sneeze, ha-a-a-choo!
Bless you! Here comes the doctor.

I feel__ sick, Help me, help me, cure me quick.

2. Doctor, doctor, I feel bad,
   My dose is rudding just like mad,
   I keep blowing, I can't stop,
   I'm all full of gleep and glop.
   Doctor, doctor, I feel bad,
   My doze is rudding just like mad.

3. Doctor, doctor, I feel rotten,
   My legs are wool, my head is cotton.
   I just ache and ache and ache,
   I can't sleep and I can't wake.
   Doctor, doctor, I feel rotten,
   Like something awful the old cat brought in.

4. Doctor, doctor, I feel crummy,
   My head fell right into my tummy.
   My eyes are bleary and I can't see
   Even Miss Piggy on TV.
   Doctor, doctor, I feel crummy,
   My head fell right into my tummy.

Holidays

WORDS AND MUSIC BY TOM GLAZER

Birthdays. Christmas. Passover. Easter. July the Fourth. Special things to eat. Fun.
Games. Stuffed turkey. Stuffed chicken. Barbecues. Picnics. I like holidays!

I like hol - i - days, you do
too._____ Hol - i - days are jol - ly days,
Pol - ly, wol - ly, gol - ly, Play with your toys and dol - ly days.

Long Time Ago

ADAPTED BY TOM GLAZER

1. Once there was a lit-tle kit-ty, White as the snow. She went out to hunt a mous-ie, Long time a go.

2. Two black eyes had lit-tle kit-ty, Black as the crow, And they spied a lit-tle mous-ie, Long time a go.

3. Four soft paws had little kitty,
   Soft as the snow,
   And they caught the little mousie,
   Long time ago.

4. Nine pearly teeth had little kitty,
   All in a row.
   And she bit the little mousie,
   Long time ago.

5. When the kitty bit the mousie,
   Mousie cried out, "Oh!"
   But she got away from kitty,
   Long time ago.

Section V

SOME GAMES

Head Bumping

Sit the child on your lap, facing you, or on some other convenient place, but very close. Bring your head quite close to the child's. Then, gently and quietly, in a soft voice say, "One, two . . . three!" and on "three," very gently touch your forehead to the child's. Repeat as often as you like.

After several head bumps (and they must be very, very gently done), vary the procedure by *not* bumping heads on "three"; instead, move your head to one side of the child's head, by way of surprise. Or touch your head against the child's arm, shoulder, et cetera.

Very young children adore this simple game and they usually laugh out loud in pleasure when the surprise takes place, when their forehead is *not* bumped. After that surprise, of course, the child will want you to resume the head bumping in the former manner.

Hands and Arms

This game is wonderful fun and wonderfully funny depending on the imagination of the participants.

The adult sits behind the child, who should be old enough to talk and walk, though even older children like this game too. The child places his arms behind his (or her, of course) back. At the same time, the adult substitutes the adult's arms for the child's, extending them from under the child's arms.

The child now begins to speak, saying anything at all. If the child does not know what to say exactly or is shy about it, the adult from behind can suggest something, or suggest some subject. As the child speaks, the adult's hands and arms make appropriate gestures, as if they were the child's own. The gestures should be exaggerated, which makes it funnier. A nose or a head can be scratched; the adult must use imagination. Of course, for best results, there should be an audience of at least one, but if no one else is present it is still entertaining, because the child can watch the adult's hands and arms making all those exaggerated gestures as if they were the child's own.

Magic Coin Tricks

Very young children, I have found, love simple magic tricks. Although I had absolutely no training as a magician, I started doing some I made up myself with my own children, quite by accident. When you see how much children love to be fooled — even by the most ridiculously simple devices — and how they also love to try to guess how it is done, and, if they are really quite young, how they actually believe in the magic as if it were real, then you can — presto change-o! — become a magician instantly. Here are a few suggestions:

Take several small but similar coins. Without the child's knowledge, place one in your pocket or in some other receptacle hidden from the child. Take one coin and show it to the child. Then say, "Watch closely." Then pretend to throw the coin. You can even say, "I'm going to throw the coin all the way across the room." The child will instinctively look in the direction you are "throwing" the coin. But instead of throwing the coin, as the child looks ahead you make a throwing motion, and in the same motion hide the coin under your other arm. It is ridiculously simple and effective and works most of the time.

Then, having "thrown" the coin, you ask the child, "Where is it, where did it go?" You may then ask the child to reach into a pocket where a second coin is hidden, or into some other receptacle or under an ashtray, and the child is delighted to retrieve the coin so magically thrown away and recovered.

A successful variant of this, which most children find entrancing, is to hide a second, similar coin in your hand, or reach into a pocket when the child's attention is diverted, again hiding the coin, and after saying several times, "Where is it, where can it be?" pretend to find it in one of the child's ears, or in his (her) hair, and so forth. This delights the child. If the child begs to know how to do the tricks, you can say, "It's a secret," or, "I don't really know," and so on. Incidentally, any simple coin trick can be done with matches or toothpicks as well, but there is something about coins and their status as money . . . If you have a steady hand and a little courage, you can practice hiding a coin in your own hand. If you experiment a little, you will see that smaller coins such as the dime or penny can be placed between two fingers where they join, and when the hand is held flat out with the fingers close together, the coin will be invisible, under the fingers. Then it is simple to work some tricks using another coin of the same denomination. For example, you can pretend to throw a second coin away (or actually throw it) with your right hand, and presto! there it is in the same hand, by passing it over your left hand (in which you have cleverly hidden a similar coin). You could very likely figure out variations based on this palming device. Remember, small children love magic and love being mystified; it doesn't take much.

The Nose-Button, Ear-Lever, Head-Machine Game

I made this up one day with my own sons and they loved it, and so do many other kids I have tried it on. Have a child press the end of your own nose. When the child does this, stick out your tongue suddenly, as if the nose were a button that causes the tongue to pop out.

Then ask the child to pull down on the lobe of one of your ears. When this is done, suddenly move your tongue to the right or left. When the child pulls on the other lobe, move the tongue the other way. Have the child press on your chin, and then shake your head back and forth. You can make up all sorts of variations of this Nose-Button, Ear-Lever, Head-Machine Game, even making funny throat sounds on some of the child's start-up actions.

Peek-a-Boo

This is so babyish, thank heaven, that you may wonder why it is included, but it is often very difficult for an adult to remember what truly simple devices delight a child. This one is for the youngest. All you do is place your hands over your face, then remove them suddenly and say, "Peek-a-boo!" Why do children love this? Probably, in my view, because they enjoy the great relief at seeing your face after it is hidden, due to the fact that a baby can, and no doubt does, experience doubt that the adult will ever return from behind the hiding hands. All children share concern that they will lose the adults they are attached to, and it is this fear-and-relief pattern, I believe, that pleases the child.

Dropping-and-Catching

This, too, I did one day accidentally, and the baby loved it. With the baby seated on your legs facing you, holding the child very firmly, suddenly open your legs, letting the child drop an inch or two, but keeping a firm hold. The sudden drop is first startling, then great fun. This must be identical to the feeling of falling and recovering we get on roller coasters.

Conclusion

In conclusion, it cannot be overemphasized that the key to a child's pleasure in games is simplicity generated by genuine pleasure in the child and love for him or her. If these are present, everything beautiful follows. But please do not be inhibited about improvising your own games; games are a form of folklore, and folklore by definition is what the people, all people, do — not extremely gifted people necessarily, like Mozart or other geniuses, but the likes of you and me.